8/05 9x 4/05

# LOS GATOS PUBLIC LIBRARY
## P.O. Box 949
## Los Gatos, CA 95031
## 408 354-6891

The registered borrower is responsible for
returning material on time and in good
condition. A fine shall be charged for each
day an item is overdue and an appropriate fee
charged to repair damage (other than normal
wear and tear). The replacement cost plus a
processing fee will be charged for any lost
item or item returned damaged beyond repair.

4.9

# Spaceships

**Amanda Davis**

The Rosen Publishing Group's

PowerKids Press™

New York

Published in 1997 by The Rosen Publishing Group, Inc.
29 East 21st Street, New York, NY 10010

First Edition

Book Design: Erin McKenna

Photo Credits: Cover and p. 10 © Jack Zehrt/FPG International Corp.; pp. 4, 11 © Telegraph Colour Library/FPG International Corp.; pp. 5, 12, 15, 18, 20 © NASA/FPG International Corp.; p. 7 © World Perspectives/FPG International Corp.; p. 8 © Earl Young/FPG International Corp.; p. 16 © T. Zimmerman/FPG International Corp.; p. 19 © FPG International Corp.; p. 22 © Robert Morrison/FPG International Corp.

Davis, Amanda.
    Spaceships / by Amanda Davis.
        p.    cm. — (Exploring Space)
    Includes index.
    Summary: Briefly discusses various spacecraft, including rockets, satellites, and space shuttles, and the jobs they perform.
     ISBN 0-8239-5063-8
     1. Space shuttles—Juvenile literature. [1. Space shuttles. 2. Space vehicles.]
    I. Title. II. Series: Davis, Amanda.  Exploring space.
TL795.5D38 1997
629.44'1—dc21

                                                                    96-54498
                                                                       CIP
                                                                        AC

Manufactured in the United States of America

# Contents

# What Is a Spaceship?

When we think of spaceships, we often think of silver ships with aliens aboard that fly from planet to planet. But these ships only exist in movies and on TV shows. Real spaceships are very big machines that may or may not carry people. They often travel around, or **orbit** (OR-bit), Earth. They are called **satellites** (SAT-el-iyts), or **exploratory** (ex-PLOR-ah-tor-ee) spaceships. There are also space shuttles, which carry astronauts to and from space. Spaceships help humans to learn new things about space and Earth.

◀ *Pioneer 10* is an example of one spaceship that doesn't carry people.

# Going to Space

Sending a spaceship into space is not easy. To leave Earth, the ships must move against Earth's **gravity** (GRA-vih-tee). This powerful, natural **force** (FORSS) causes objects to be **attracted** (uh-TRAK-ted) to each other. Gravity keeps people, cars, and houses attached to Earth.

To overcome Earth's gravity, a spaceship must reach a speed of almost 25,000 miles per hour. An airplane only goes about 500 miles per hour!

To go all the way into space, we have to use the most powerful engines we have. These are called **rocket engines** (ROK-et EN-jinz).

Rocket engines are attached to the spaceship ▶ and help it travel into space.

# Rockets

Rockets are tall, thin machines that can carry a spaceship into space. Huge tanks of **fuel** (FYOOL) and **oxygen** (AHK-sih-jen) take up most of the room inside a rocket.

The fuel and oxygen mix together at the bottom end of the rocket. When the two combine, a very large amount of hot gas shoots out the bottom of the rocket in a huge explosion. The force of the gas causes the rocket to lift off the **surface** (SER-fiss) of Earth.

◀ A rocket gets its power from the fuel and oxygen inside of it.

# Satellites

Satellites are small spaceships that orbit Earth and allow us to do amazing things. Some receive signals in space from one spot on Earth and send the signals back down to another spot. This all happens in seconds. These signals are how long distance phone calls are made.

Other satellites take pictures of Earth from space. Pictures from weather satellites help us to know the paths of storms and hurricanes before they hit the ground.

Right now thousands of satellites are orbiting Earth, helping people learn all sorts of things.

Satellites help us learn more about things on Earth. ▶

# Exploratory Spaceships

We also use spaceships to study the **solar system** (SOH-ler SIS-tem) and the **universe** (YOO-nih-vers).

In 1977, we sent the *Voyager 1* and *Voyager 2* spaceships to the outer planets of our solar system. The photos they sent back showed us Jupiter, the biggest planet in our solar system. We now know that Jupiter has rings around it and one of its moons has volcanoes on it!

Now *Voyager 1* and *Voyager 2* are on their way into deep space outside our solar system. They will send us information about this unknown area of the universe for another 30 years.

◀ Scientists first built a model of exactly what the *Voyager* spaceship would look like.

# Mars

Scientists are now working on a plan to collect rocks from Mars, another planet in our solar system. In 1996, scientists studied a rock that fell to Earth from Mars 13,000 years ago. They found **fossils** (FOS-ulz) of tiny living things in this rock. This led them to believe that there might be life on other planets.

In 2001, a ship carrying a **vehicle** (VEE-ih-kul) called *Rocky 7* will land on Mars. This jeep-like machine will go over the surface of Mars and collect rocks.

Two years later, another spaceship will land on Mars to collect the rocks from *Rocky 7*. Then the spaceship will bring the rocks back to Earth. Scientists will look for more signs of life in these rocks.

Does the surface of Mars hold the answers to whether there is life on other planets? ▶

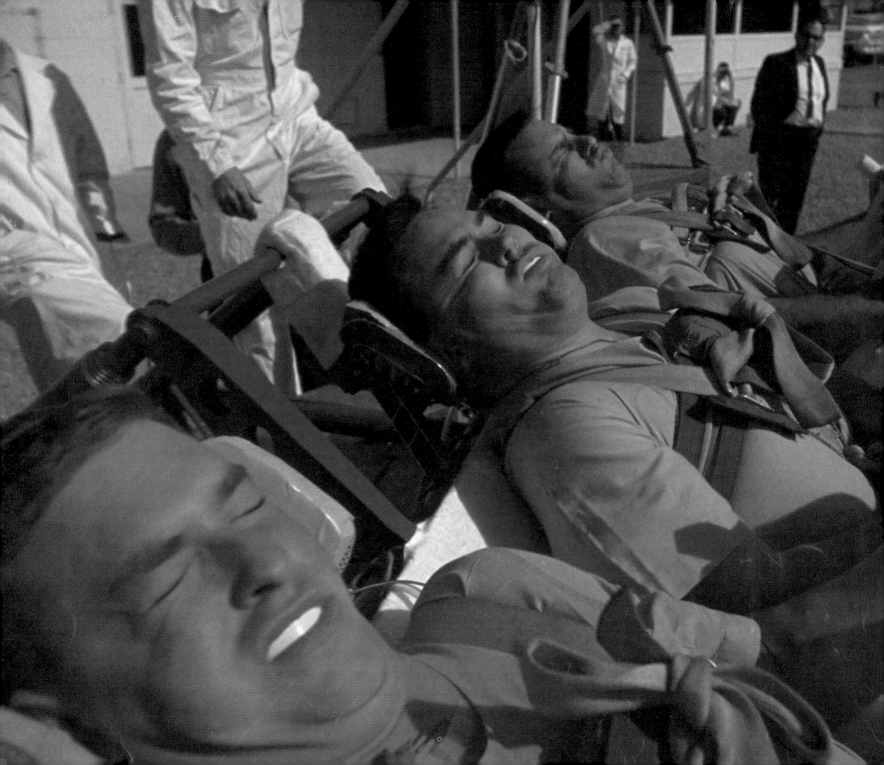

# Humans in Space

When we put people in a spaceship, it's much different than just sending a satellite into space. **Astronauts** (AH-stro-nots) need air to breathe, food to eat, and room to move around. These things aren't necessary for satellites and exploratory spaceships.

The most important thing for humans traveling in space is safety. We have to be sure that a spaceship with people on it is sturdy so our astronauts come back to Earth in good health.

**SPACE FACT**

The first astronauts had to be under 5 feet, 11 inches tall because of the small size of the cabins in the first spaceships.

◄ Astronauts go through many safety tests before they travel into space.

# The Moon

One of the most exciting moments in history was when we sent astronauts to the moon. *Apollo 11* was lifted into space by the rocket *Saturn 5*. This rocket was as tall as a skyscraper!

*Saturn 5* had to be powerful enough to lift all the equipment needed to get the astronauts to the moon and back. This included a buggy that the astronauts drove on the surface of the moon.

**SPACE FACT**

On July 20, 1969, Neil Armstrong became the first man to walk on the moon.

Americans were proud to see their flag planted on the moon. ▶

# The Space Shuttle

The space shuttle looks like a giant airplane. The first one, called *Columbia*, went into space in 1981.

Before the space shuttle, spaceships carrying people could only be used once. The astronauts came back to Earth in **landing modules** (LAN-ding MOD-yoolz). The ships they left behind were either destroyed in space or sent further out into space, never to be seen again.

But the space shuttle is different. It takes off like a regular spaceship, but it can return to Earth and land on a runway just like an airplane!

◀ A space shuttle can be used again, just like an airplane or helicopter.

# Space Shuttle Missions

Thirteen space shuttles have traveled into space. Space shuttle astronauts do **experiments** (ex-PEER-ih-mentz) in space. They even fix broken satellites!

Sadly, one space shuttle had a terrible accident. In 1986, the space shuttle *Challenger* exploded just after liftoff. All the astronauts on board died.

But the rest of the shuttles continue to explore space. Scientists and astronauts are using the space shuttle to build the International Space Station, which will be the biggest space station ever built. The building won't be finished until the year 2002.

# Glossary

**astronaut** (AH-stro-not)  A person who is trained to travel in space.

**attract** (uh-TRAKT)  When one thing automatically moves closer to another.

**experiment** (ex-PEER-ih-ment)  A test done on something to learn more about it.

**exploratory** (ex-PLOR-ah-tor-ee)  When something is used to study the unknown.

**force** (FORSS)  Something in nature that causes action.

**fossil** (FOS-ul)  An imprint found in rock of a plant or an animal that lived long ago.

**fuel** (FYOOL)  A liquid that is used to make machines work.

**gravity** (GRA-vih-tee)  A force between two objects that causes them to be attracted to each other.

**landing modules** (LAN-ding MOD-yoolz)  Small spaceships used to carry astronauts from their spaceships back to Earth

**orbit** (OR-bit)  How one thing circles around another thing.

**oxygen** (AHK-sih-jen)  A gas that is needed to cause the explosion in rocket engines to lift a spaceship into space. Humans also need oxygen to breathe.

**rocket engine** (ROK-et EN-jin)  A powerful engine used to lift spaceships into space.

**satellite** (SAT-el-iyt)  An object in space that orbits a larger object. Many human-made satellites orbit Earth.

**solar system** (SOH-ler SIS-tem)  A group of planets and other objects in space that circle a star.

**surface** (SER-fiss)  The top of something.

**universe** (YOO-nih-vers)  Everything that exists. Our solar system is part of the universe.

**vehicle** (VEE-ih-kul)  A machine used to move things around.

# Index